BASIC ✳ ESSENTIALS®
ARCHERY

A **FALCON** GUIDE®

BASIC ESSENTIALS® SERIES

BASIC ✸ ESSENTIALS®
ARCHERY

BETH L. HABEISHI

and

STEPHANIE MALLORY

FALCON®

GUILFORD, CONNECTICUT
HELENA, MONTANA

AN IMPRINT OF THE GLOBE PEQUOT PRESS

_A_ FALCON GUIDE ®

Copyright © 2004 by The Globe Pequot Press

Falcon, FalconGuide, and Basic Essentials are registered trademarks of The Globe Pequot Press.

All photos are courtesy of the authors, Beth L. Habeishi and Stephanie Mallory.
Text and page design by Casey Shain
Illustrations by Diane Blasius

Library of Congress Cataloging-in-Publication Data
Habeishi, Beth L.
    Basic essentials: Archery/Beth L. Habeishi and Stephanie Mallory; [illustrations by Diane Blasius].—1st ed.
        p. cm. — (A FalconGuide) (Basic essentials series)
    Includes index.
    ISBN 0-7627-3045-5
    1. Archery. I. Title: Archery. II. Mallory, Stephanie. III. Title. IV. Falcon guide.

GV1185.H214 2004
799.3'2—dc22   2003057112

Manufactured in the United States of America
First Edition/First Printing

The Globe Pequot Press assumes no liability for accidents happening to, or injuries sustained by, readers who engage in the activities described in this book.

Contents

Acknowledgments

This book would not have been possible without the help of the following people: Sean Alcazar, certified personal trainer with Fitness Together; Jeff Chastain, archery expert at Arlie's Great Outdoors in Birmingham, Alabama; Joella Bates, archery instructor and professional archery competitor; Michele Crummer, finance director at Muzzy Products Corporation; Tess Randle Jolly, freelance writer/photographer and archery instructor with the "Becoming an Outdoors Woman" program; Robert and Hilda Pittman, owners of White Oak Plantation in Tuskegee, Alabama; Bob Shebaylo, president of Champion Bow Company; and John Sloan, freelance writer and eastern editor of *Bow and Arrow Hunting Magazine.*

Introduction

People are drawn to archery for a variety of reasons. Some want to discover the rich heritage of their ancestors who relied on their archery skills for both survival and entertainment. Some like the challenge of perfecting their form and consistently hitting the bull's-eye. Others enjoy archery's quiet simplicity, the fluid movements of the draw, and the silent flight of an arrow. And many savor the camaraderie of others who share a passion for the sport. For whatever reason you decide to pursue archery, the sport can provide you with a lifetime of enjoyment.

No matter one's age, gender, or physical limitations, anyone can participate in archery. Unlike sports that rely heavily on physical ability, archery depends more on a person's ability to concentrate and focus on the task at hand. Mental discipline, instinct, and self-confidence also play significant roles in one's proficiency. Drawing a bow and shooting an arrow is not a thoughtless process but one that requires precise calculations and intense concentration. Nevertheless, instinct and natural talent can give someone an advantage. Self-confidence can also put an archer ahead of the game. Positive thinking often results in successful shooting. And you may notice that shooting skills and self-confidence increase as time progresses.

No matter how quickly or slowly you advance in your pursuit of archery, always set realistic goals for yourself. Although you should constantly challenge yourself, don't get discouraged if others seem to develop their skills more quickly. Archery is a continually evolving sport as techniques and equipment improve, and you have a lifetime to learn and perfect your skills.

Throughout the learning process, archery can reveal many things about your temperament, your character, and your personality. As you participate in the sport, you will realize how determined you are to accomplish your goals, what methods you use to deal with frustrations, what steps you are willing to take to overcome obstacles, how patient you are with others, and how hard you're willing to work to experience success.

Who knows where archery may take you?

Archery can provide you with many new opportunities depending on the level of your involvement. With archery, your options are limitless, whether you choose to be a backyard archer or a nationwide competitor. Who knows where archery may take you? Your archery skills may earn you a scholarship to a major university or win you a gold medal at the Olympic Games. Or the sport may simply provide you with a new hobby to share with your family members and friends. No matter the level to which you take archery, you undoubtedly will enjoy this ancient and honorable pastime.

As with any sport, archery requires practice and dedication. To truly appreciate archery one must learn the essentials of the sport. This book, *Basic Essentials of Archery,* will guide you through the necessary steps required to get started. After you read this book thoroughly, keep it as a reference as you study, learn, and practice this discipline.

Editor's note: Key terms have been italicized in this book. For a useful abbreviated definition of each of these terms, please turn to the Glossary at the back of the book.

The History of Archery

I magine for a moment someone with a bow and arrow. Any number of images may come to mind. Robin Hood, the notorious outlaw and accomplished archer, is one of the most popular choices. The archer-god, Phoebus Apollo, or the mischievous Cupid may also come to mind. But what about a Native American, an African tribesman, or even a Japanese samurai? Did you picture a family of camouflaged hunters with bows in hand moving cautiously through the woods, searching for a source of food? Did you imagine an army of medieval knights engaged in fierce battle, firing enough arrows to blacken the sky?

Archery, one of the oldest arts still practiced today, has played an integral role in history. And until the development of modern firearms, the bow and arrow was the weapon of choice for more than 50,000 years in almost every corner of the world. The pages of history are filled with images of men and women—from ancient Egyptians to Pygmy bushmen—armed with their bows and arrows. These men and women practiced archery to hunt for food, protect their homes, and fight in some of history's most significant battles. Thousands of years later, people all over the world still enjoy the sport of archery. So when you pick up a bow and shoot your first arrow, remember that you are participating in an activity that has been around for centuries.

Origin and Development of Archery

Primitive man first made use of the bow and arrow as a weapon. Based on the discovery of crudely fashioned bows and arrows dating back hundreds of thousands of years, researchers have concluded that ancient humans constructed these weapons from various raw materials and used them to safeguard their homes and hunt more efficiently.

Although using a spear or a knife was effective, taking down enemies or prey from a distance with a bow was easier and safer. The shapes and sizes of the earliest bows are unknown, as worn-out or broken bows probably ended up on the fire, were used for something else, or were simply discarded.

Soon the bow and arrow began to play an important role in war. Archery as a means of hunting and combat is prominently mentioned throughout the Old Testament; as archery continued to evolve and develop, more and more civilizations began using the bow and arrow to defend themselves and conquer their enemies. For example, the ancient Egyptians established the bow as their weapon of choice around 3500 B.C. They constructed their arrowheads from flint and bronze and used bows that were almost as tall as they were.

Around 1800 B.C. the Assyrians developed the shorter recurve bow. This bow was stronger, lighter, and smaller than the Egyptian bow, and the Assyrians gained a distinct advantage in battle with its development. Archery in the Middle East remained superior for many centuries, as these skilled archers demonstrated by successfully fighting off the warriors of European civilizations. In 1200 B.C. the Hittites, who also used recurve bows, developed the skill of shooting from moving chariots in battle. And around A.D. 500 the Romans, formerly known as inferior archers, began to draw their bows at eye level rather than chest level, giving their shots more accuracy. Greeks, Huns, Persians, Parthians, Mongols, and Turks were also among the civilizations recognized for their innovations in bow-and-arrow construction and military strategy.

No one knows for certain when archery first appeared in England. Invading armies most likely introduced the bow to Britain at several points in its history. However, before the reign of William the Conqueror, the bow appears to have been regarded primarily as a hunting tool, and archers played little—if any—role in battle. England ultimately adopted the bow as its primary weapon of defense against massed cavalry and designed short bows for use on horseback and for shooting at distant targets. But in A.D. 1066 the Normans, using longbows, defeated the English at the Battle of Hastings. The English wisely adapted the Norman bow and abandoned their shorter, weaker, less-accurate bows. Their new bows had draw weights of 60 to 120 pounds and were often used at ranges up to 250 yards. In the fourteenth century, the English used these longbows to overcome frightful odds against mounted, fully armored French knights. And some of the most renowned ballads and legends of this time, such as the tales of Robin Hood, attest to the skills of the English with their longbows.

The bow remained the most effective and accurate weapon for thousands of years, until the development of firearms in the sixteenth century led to a decline in the popularity of archery as a tool of war. Still, archery remained a favorite pastime—especially in England under the reign of King Henry VIII, who prompted the creation of several archery organizations and the establishment of archery as a competitive sport.

When the Europeans began colonizing America, they incorporated some of what they learned of Native American bow styles into their own approach to bow construction. Native American tribes of the Plains especially became known for their amazing speed and accuracy with short arrows and short bows from 3 feet to 4 feet long. Riding on galloping horses, they could fire a handful of arrows in mere seconds and easily overtake a grazing herd of buffalo or an unprepared group of soldiers. But Native American bows were small and weak, with draw weights ranging from twenty-eight to seventy pounds. To deliver an effective shot, Native American archers had to come dangerously close to their targets or their prey.

Archery remained only a recreational activity in the newly born United States of America, and many people lost interest in the sport altogether. After the Civil War, however, a new interest in archery developed. When the victorious Union banned former Confederate soldiers from using firearms, they turned to the bow for hunting and recreation. Its new-found popularity led to the creation of the National Archery Association of the United States. The National Field Archery Association was founded shortly after as a response to the rising popularity of field archery and bow hunting.

Archery made its debut as an Olympic sport at the Paris Olympics of 1900 and appeared again in the 1904, 1908, and 1920 games. But due to the absence of an organized set of rules, the sport did not appear in the Olympics again for fifty-two years. The Fédération Internationale de Tir à l'Arc (FITA), founded in the 1930s, played a significant role in the reintroduction of competitive archery to the world. When the organization developed the universal rules for the sport, international competition advanced quickly, and archery returned as an Olympic sport in 1972.

Since the 1970s advances in technology have led to the creation of faster arrows, more consistent bows, and higher quality equipment. This new equipment far "outshoots" all previous equipment in range, accuracy, and weight and has made archery more popular and more prevalent all over the world.

Archery Heroes and Legends

A movie star, an outlaw, a literary figure, and an Early American author. What do these four individuals have in common? Whether fact or fiction, each of these talented men mastered the bow and arrow and became archery heroes and legends in their own cultures and throughout the world.

Howard Hill: Howard Hill, renowned for his exceptional archery skills, became involved with the film industry as an archery consultant and performed the shooting scenes in eight movies including *The Adventures of Robin Hood,* starring Errol Flynn. During his lifetime Hill earned many awards including the Maurice Thompson Medal of Honor, the National Archery Association's most prestigious award. He was also one of the first archers inducted into the Archery Hall of Fame. Even at the age of sixty-two, Hill could draw and shoot a seventy-five-pound compound bow with ease. He never liked to use sights or other mechanisms on his bows. He felt they took away from the challenge of the bow. Also, he preferred to keep his bow free of anything that might hinder its maneuverability and accuracy. And although Hill was exceptionally talented with everything from a simple recurve to a complex cable-and-pulley (compound) bow, he believed that much of the modern equipment detracted from the romance of the ancient sport of archery.

Robin Hood: The history of archery cannot be told without mentioning the legendary Robin Hood. For more than 600 years, stories of Robin Hood have been passed down from generation to generation. The romance and the intrigue surrounding this outlaw who stole from the rich to give to the poor are still a part of his captivating tale. From the first time people spoke of him, Robin Hood was believed to have been a real person. However, although many have speculated about this legendary archer, his identity remains unknown to this day. In Robin's time few people could read or write, so they learned about Robin and his band of merry men through the songs of wandering minstrels who incorporated fact and fiction into whatever tale they may be telling. No one has ever provided authentic records of Robin Hood's activities, but five of the oldest surviving ballads tell us much of what is known about his legend. One of the most familiar tales recounts how a disguised Robin won an important archery contest by shooting a second arrow straight through the first arrow he'd already shot into the target's center. The shooting of an arrow end to end is still referred to as a "Robin Hood."

Odysseus: The literary figure Odysseus from Homer's *Iliad* and *Odyssey* was also a legendary archer. As a king of Ithaca, Odysseus was a strong and valiant warrior who fought in the Trojan War and wandered for ten years afterward. While Odysseus was gone, his wife, Penelope, discouraged and distracted a number of suitors, hoping that her husband would soon return. However, when Odysseus did not return, she decided that she must surrender to the suitors, so she proposed a test to settle who shall have her hand in marriage: The man who could string Odysseus's bow and shoot an arrow through twelve small rings would marry her. When every suitor failed to even string the massive bow, a disguised Odysseus picked up the bow, strung it, and shot an arrow through every ring. Because of his incredible archery skills, Odysseus regained his wife and kingdom.

J. Maurice Thompson: As the author of *The Witchery of Archery,* Maurice Thompson played an important role in the resurgence of archery in the United States after the Civil War. When firearms were prohibited in much of the South, Maurice and his brother, William, took up archery. Learning their skills from Native Americans in Florida, the two brothers became accomplished hunters and bowmen. They also became founding members of the National Archery Association in 1879. Thompson's book helped spread enthusiasm for archery during his time and still continues to captivate people today. As he wrote: "So long as the new moon returns in the heaven a bent, beautiful bow, so long will the fascination of archery keep hold of the hearts of men."

Significant Dates in the History of Archery

◆ **Pre-25,000 B.C.:** Early man may have invented the bow and arrow in Africa, possibly as early as 50,000 B.C., where the first stone arrowheads were discovered.

◆ **25,000–18,000 B.C.:** Man begins using fire-hardened points on arrows. They shaped flint arrowheads to a point and inserted them into a slot on the arrow and tied them with sinew. They also tied feathers with sinew to the arrow shafts.

◆ **5000 B.C.:** Egyptians used the longbow for hunting and warfare.

◆ **2800 B.C.:** Composite bows, those made from composite material or separate pieces, first appear.

◆ **1200–700 B.C.:** Assyrian archers shot from chariots while the charioteer held a shield for protection.

◆ **360 B.C.:** Macedonian archers on horseback supported heavy cavalry in battle.

◆ **A.D. 434:** Huns (led by Atilla) used composite recurve bows from horseback against opposing armies with deadly effect.

◆ **A.D. 1099:** Crusaders consisted mainly of desert horsemen armed with composite bows and scimitars.

◆ **A.D. 1208:** Mongols (led by Genghis Khan) were expert mounted archers who used high saddles and stirrups that allowed them to shoot in any direction. They used composite bows and released the bowstring with a thumb ring that increased the killing range of the bow to 300 yards.

◆ **A.D. 1500–1550:** Ballads about Robin Hood "Lyttell Geste of Robyn Hode," "Robin and the Knight," "Robin, Little John, and the Sheriff," "Robin and the King," and "Robin Hood's Death" were written and passed along in song.

◆ **A.D. 1508:** English rulers prohibited the use of crossbows in England to increase the use of longbows.

◆ **A.D. 1520:** The musket, which will ultimately replace the bow as a weapon of war, was invented.

◆ **A.D. 1673:** Archers in Yorkshire, England, established the archery tournament known as the Ancient Scorton Silver Arrow Contest. (It is the oldest archery tournament still held today.)

◆ **A.D. 1676:** The Royal Company of Archers first practiced clout archery using longbows to shoot at a thirty-one-inch diameter target at distances between 180 to 240 yards.

◆ **A.D. 1828:** United Bowmen of Philadelphia was founded. (This is the first and oldest of any U.S. archery organizations still in existence today.)

◆ **A.D. 1879:** National Archery Association (NAA) was founded in Crawfordsville, Indiana.

◆ **A.D. 1900:** Archery was first introduced in the Olympic games—also in 1904, 1908, and 1920. (Women were allowed to compete in the archery events in 1904 and 1908.)

◆ **A.D. 1931:** The Fédération Internationale de Tir à l'Arc (FITA) was formed.

◆ **A.D. 1946:** Doug Easton developed a process for manufacturing aluminum arrow shafts.

◆ **A.D. 1939:** National Field Archery Association (NFFA) was founded.

◆ **A.D. 1966:** International Field Archery Association (IFFA) was founded.

◆ **A.D. 1966:** H.W. Allen, a Missouri bowhunter, was credited with the invention of the compound bow.

◆ **A.D. 1970:** Compound bows and release aids made their national debut, and the NFAA accepted them in competitions.

◆ **A.D. 1972:** Archery reappeared in the Munich Olympic games as an event for both men and women.

Equipment and Gear

As a newcomer to the sport of archery, you're excited about learning all you can about archery and especially about practicing your new skills. But don't run out and buy the first bow you see. You need to take careful steps in selecting your archery equipment. Before purchasing your first bow, seek the advice of a knowledgeable salesperson or an experienced archer.

Common Bows: Recurve, Compound, and Longbow

You most likely want to choose from the three most commonly used bow types: the recurve bow, the compound bow, and the longbow. Although each type of bow is different in appearance, all bows have similar basic characteristics. All bows store their energy in the limbs; they all have handles or risers that are attached to the limbs; they all use strings to fire the arrow from the bow. Although you can have a lot of fun learning to shoot all types of bows, many people prefer the high-end technology of the compound bow. But many professionals suggest that beginning archers start with a quality recurve bow. When making the decision to buy your own equipment, first decide on the style of archery that appeals to you. If you've decided not to join an archery club, and you have a sufficiently large, safe space where you can practice your archery skills, then you can buy an inexpensive fiberglass bow and wooden or fiberglass arrows. However, if you plan to shoot at club or competition level, you may want to purchase higher-quality equipment. Just remember that the basic archery equipment you should have to begin includes a bow, a dozen or so matched arrows, an arm guard, a finger tab, and a quiver.

General Bow Terminology

Before you go out shopping for a bow, you should become familiar with general bow terminology.

◆ **Arrow rest:** A small, tablike shelf where the arrow rests. You don't have to shoot the arrow from the rest. You can shoot it from the shelf. But a proper length arrow will bend and shift when you release it. If you shoot it from a properly installed arrow rest underneath a properly installed nock locator, it will clear the bow without friction, resulting in a more accurate shot.

◆ **Arrow shelf:** The small shelf where the arrow sits when the archer aims, draws, and releases the arrow.

◆ **Back:** The side of the bow facing away from the archer and toward the target.

◆ **Bowstring:** The cord to which the arrows are fitted. The string must not stretch under normal environmental conditions because that would change the bow's pull weight and make consistency impossible.

◆ **Bow window:** The recessed area above the bow handle or grip.

◆ **Draw weight:** The amount of effort (or pounds of pull) required to fully draw back a bow.

◆ **Face:** The side of the bow facing the archer.

◆ **Handle/grip:** The place where the archer holds the bow between the two bow limbs.

◆ **Limb:** Part of the bow from the riser to the tip.

◆ **Nocking point:** The place on the string where the arrow is fitted.

◆ **Nock locator:** The place on the bowstring marked (perhaps by a small plastic ring) to let the archer know where to nock his arrow on the string.

◆ **Riser:** The handle area of the bow. The side facing the target is called the back; the side near the string, the face.

◆ **Sight:** A mechanical device placed on the bow with which the archer can aim directly at the target.

◆ **Stabilizer:** An additional weight mounted on a bow, usually extending some distance from the handle, used to minimize undesirable torques of the bowstring on release.

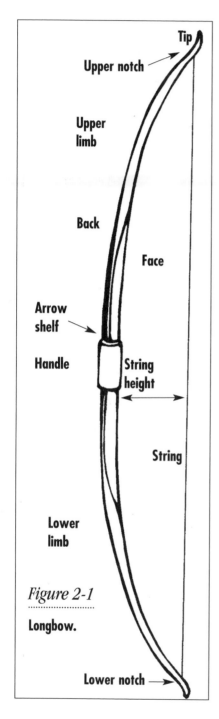

Upper notch

Tip

Upper limb

Back

Face

Arrow shelf

Handle

String height

String

Lower limb

Figure 2-1

Longbow.

Lower notch

The Longbow

In recent years the popularity of the traditional styles of archery has increased. The traditional shape of the *longbow* comes from that of the bows European archers used in the Middle Ages, though its shape hasn't changed greatly since its invention approximately 9000–6,000 B.C. An off-the-shelf longbow generally measures 72 inches tall and comes in a range of draw weights; right-handed and left-handed archers can use the same bow. But these bows have very little leverage because the limbs only make one motion, which prevents them from storing much energy. The longbow has no recurves, pulleys, or cams, unlike the recurve and the compound bows, making it the least-expensive model. In addition, when you shoot a longbow, the arrow always has to sit off center of the handle. Because longbows have no sight apparatus, archers usually have to compensate by shooting this bow in an instinctive manner from the right or left side of the handle.

Recurve or Olympic Bow

Traditional archers favor the *recurve bow* because of its reliability, smooth draw, and compactibility. The only bow allowed in Olympic competition, the recurve bow descends directly from antique bows. Recurves differ from antique bows only in the materials used to construct them. The tips of the working limbs of the recurve bow bend backward in the opposite direction from the draw when at rest. This design allows the bow to harness more power when drawn and to store and release energy more efficiently, as well as increase velocity in the arrow as the arrow begins to leave the string. The bow handles (risers) are made of aluminum alloys and machined for strength and lightness. Some lower-cost bows have wooden risers, as do some expensive handmade bows. The bow limbs are generally constructed of man-made materials, such as fiberglass, carbon, and synthetic foam. The force required to pull a recurve bow increases directly with the distance pulled. The recurve bow is a more efficient model than the longbow. Instead of only having one motion when drawn, the recurve has two. When drawn, the limbs of the recurve uncurl in two different directions and return to their original positions when the archer releases the bowstring. The amount of recurve can vary from a slight curve at each tip to a total curve causing the entire working limb of the bow to bend backward to the point that the two tips will actually touch when unstrung.

When buying a recurve bow, make sure you choose one with the correct draw length and draw weight for you. The *draw weight* (known as poundage) refers to the effort required to draw the arrow to a specific distance. So a bow described as being "26# @28" means it requires 26 pounds of pull to draw the arrow to 28 inches. Choose a bow weight you can draw, hold, and release with comfort.

Your height and reach determine the

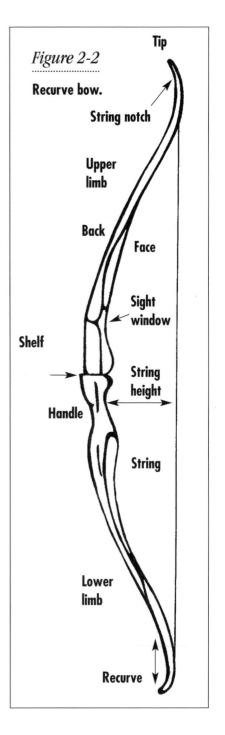

Figure 2-2

Recurve bow.

Tip
String notch
Upper limb
Back
Face
Sight window
Shelf
String height
Handle
String
Lower limb
Recurve

Specific Recurve Terminology

A few key terms are specific to the recurve bow.

◆ **Pivot point:** The place where you grip the bow between your thumb and the rest of your fingers. The place on the bow's handle that is farthest away from the string.

◆ **Recurve:** The forward curves on the limb tips of a recurve bow.

Recurve bow.

length of the bow you need. You should start by measuring your *draw length,* the distance between the nocking point on the bowstring and the grip of the bow at full draw. You can obtain an estimate of your draw length by measuring from your breastbone to your fingertips with your arms held out straight in front of you and your fingertips touching. Make sure you get the correct length of bow. A bow that is too long for your draw length will cause you to struggle when pulling it. One that is too short will prevent you from performing your best. Use the chart that follows to help determine the size bow you will need.

DRAW LENGTH	BOW LENGTH
under 24 inches	60–64 inches
25–26 inches	65–66 inches
27–28 inches	67–68 inches
29 inches or more	69–70 inches

Compound Bow

Once only used for hunting, this powerful bow has gained in popularity among archers who prefer it for recreational use. The most efficient and complex bow model, the *compound bow* has an off-center cam (sort of pulley) at the end of each limb. Rotating the pulley with the longer radius takes greater force than rotating the part with the shorter radius. In other words you need more force to pull the bowstring halfway than you need to pull it from the halfway point all the way back. The term *let-off* describes this lessening of the force required to pull the bowstring past the halfway mark. Let-off allows archers to use bows that shoot arrows with more pounds of thrust. For example, if an archer shoots a fifty-pound compound bow with 50 percent let-off, he or she will actually pull only twenty-five pounds at full draw. However, the arrow still receives fifty pounds of thrust, so the arrow accelerates faster and faster once released. The compound bow operates opposite of other types of bows, which tend to generate their maximum force at full draw and minimum force undrawn. Many consider this fast, compact bow easier to learn. Choose a compound bow with a range that includes your draw length and draw weight. Most bows adjust to ensure an exact match.

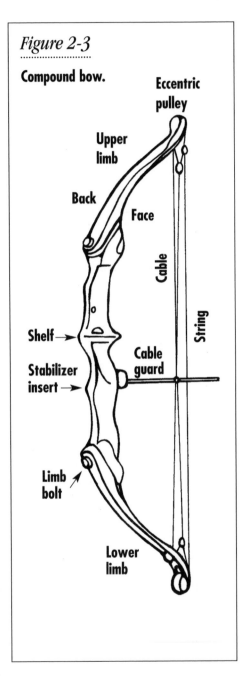

Figure 2-3

Compound bow.

Specific Compound Terminology

The more complex compound bow has a few additional parts.

◆ **Cam:** A small oval-shaped wheel mounted on each tip of each limb of the bow. The cam provides the archers with let-off.

◆ **Eccentric pulley:** These pulleys have the same purpose as the cams. Like the cams, they are on each tip of each limb, but unlike them, pulleys are round and not oval.

◆ **Stabilizer insert:** A place where a stabilizer or weighted rod can be attached to the bow. A stabilizer helps to keep the bow from moving from side to side when the archer releases the bowstring.

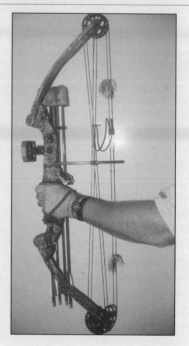

Compound bow.

Arrows

Just as you have a variety of bow types from which to choose, you also can select from numerous arrow types and lengths. Always make sure the thickness and length of your arrows match your bow weight and draw length. For instance, the average adult male may use a 28-inch arrow, the average adult female and/or teenager may use a 26-inch arrow, and the average preteen may use a 25-inch arrow. You can determine your proper arrow length by placing the nock end of an arrow in the middle of your chest. Hold the arrow between your hands and extend your arms with your palms together. The point of a proper length arrow should extend past your fingertips by approximately half an inch. You also can go to your local sporting goods store and ask an archery expert for help. The store should have the equipment necessary to determine your proper arrow length.

Arrows can be made from wood, fiberglass, aluminum, aluminum-carbon, and carbon. Cedar, pine, and Douglas fir arrows are mainly used for longbows. And because they are the least expensive of all arrow

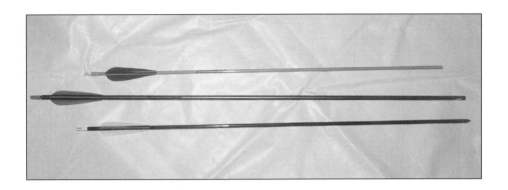

Arrows in different materials and lengths.

types, beginning archers may use them with compound or recurve bows as well. Fiberglass arrows last longer than wooden arrows, come in various sizes, and can be manufactured more uniformly than wooden arrows. Although more expensive, aluminum arrows are more durable and more accurate than wooden or fiberglass arrows. Carbon and aluminum-carbon arrows fly faster and provide less crosswind resistance, thus making them more useful in long-distance outdoor archery. If you need help selecting the type of arrow you should use with your bow, seek the advice of an archery expert or instructor.

In addition, depending on the type of archery you pursue, you can choose from six basic point types: bird, blunt, broadhead, fish, field, and target. The bird, blunt, broadhead, and fish points are used most often for hunting, while the field and target points are used most often for target archery. For example, in target archery the front end of an arrow is weighted and tipped with a small, light target point designed to penetrate a short distance into the target butt. The other end of the arrow features a nock, a plastic cap glued or attached to the end of the arrow. The nocking point grips the string until flung loose, and it provides a protection for the shaft by deflecting hits from later incoming arrows. Arrows in the recurve-bow events can travel in excess of 150 miles per hour (mph), while arrows shot from compound bows can fly in excess of 225 mph.

The arrow usually has three fletchings, one of which (the index feather) is a different color from the other two. The nock is installed gripping the string perpendicular to the odd fletch, so that the other fletchings both brush the riser equally, minimally disturbing the arrow's flight. Fletchings can be made of plastic feathers or solid vanes and come in a variety of shapes, lengths, and colors. Many serious target archers

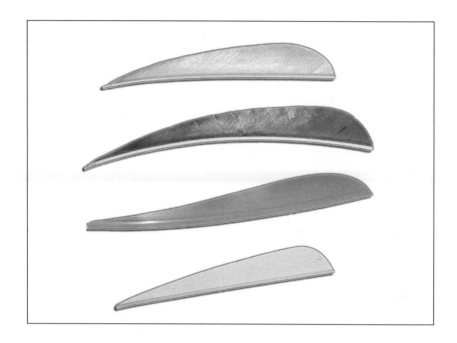

Different types of fletchings.

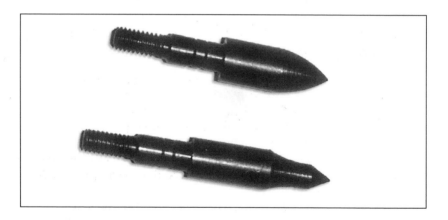

Field and target points.

prefer molded rubber or plastic vanes to the traditional feathers because vanes aren't affected by rainy weather. Fletchings glued to the arrow sometimes cause the shaft to spin around its long dimension. Although fletchings further stabilize the arrow's flight, they cause the arrow to drop slightly before hitting the target because of the additional weight.

Arrow Terminology

Even arrows are made up of a number of parts. Here are some basic terms you'll need to know.

◆ **Crest:** Colored bands or markings close to the fletchings.

◆ **Fletchings:** The feathers attached at the rear of the arrow. Fletchings are most often made of soft plastic. Feather fletchings can be used, but they are less durable than plastic fletchings. Usually three fletchings are glued to the shaft near the rear of the arrow. They are usually angled to make the arrow spin as it flies so that the arrow has a more stable, straight flight.

◆ **Flight:** An individual feather that makes up part of the fletchings.

◆ **Index feather:** The feather mounted on the shaft of the arrow at a right angle; often of a distinctive color.

◆ **Nock:** The groove cut into the end of an arrow usually made of rigid plastic. Nocks will clip onto the bowstring and keep the arrow in place. Nocks come in six different sizes to suit the range of diameters of arrows.

◆ **Point:** The sharp end of the arrow that penetrates the target.

◆ **Shaft:** The body of an arrow.

Other Archery Equipment

There's more to archery equipment than just bows and arrows. Every sport has its accessories and safety gear.

Arm guard: Archers wear an arm guard on the forearm of the bow arm to protect it from the bowstring as it is released and to minimize effect of any contact of the string to the arm. They are often made of reinforced leather or plastic.

Finger tab: Many archers wear this protective tab over the first three fingers of the draw hand to protect their fingers and to improve the smoothness of the release. Without a finger tab the friction of the bowstring during release and the pressure of drawing and holding the bowstring can damage flesh and create calluses on the fingertips and hand. Most finger tabs are made from plastic or leather.

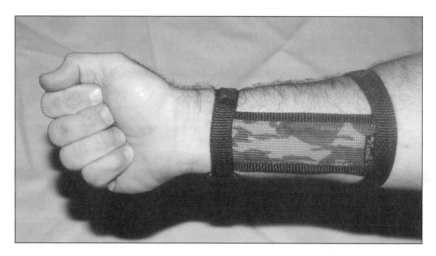

Arm guard.

Kisser button: This small horizontal disk attaches to the bowstring above the nock locator. When touched to the lips at full draw, the kisser button helps to maintain proper anchor position before releasing the arrow.

Peep sight: The archer lines up his shot by looking through the hole in this small plastic or metal disk that attaches between the strands of the bowstring.

Quiver: Most archers choose to carry their arrows in quivers, cases that protect the arrows. Modern bows, especially compounds and recurves, may have quivers that attach to the bows. There are three basic types of quivers: the ground quiver, the belt quiver, and the holster belt quiver. A ground quiver is made from a steel rod and is spiked into the ground to hold the bow and arrows. A belt quiver and a holster quiver hold the arrows on the archer. You may also use an arrow stand not only for shooting, but also as an arrow and bow rack when not shooting. These stands are generally portable and can be carried onto or off the line easily.

Release aid: Most compound shooters use a mechanical device to release the arrow. They use jaws or a loop of string to hold and release the bowstring by depressing the trigger. There are many different types of release aids. The basic types include the chonco type, which is held in the hand and triggered with the index finger; the finger type, which is held in the fingers and triggered with the thumb or little finger; and the wrist type, which wraps around the wrist and is triggered with the index finger.

Peep sight.

Quiver.

Release aid.

Do Your Research

You should do some research and become familiar with a few key concepts before you purchase your archery equipment. Understanding these concepts will help you purchase the most suitable equipment for you.

First, you need to know about forgiveness, a bow's built-in ability to compensate for the flaws in your shooting form—or at least not amplify them. Several factors affect forgiveness, such as axle-to-axle length, which is the length of the bow measured from the centerline of the axles. The trend today has moved toward shorter lengths. Generally, a shorter bow will shoot faster, but it will be less forgiving. Another factor affecting forgiveness is brace height, which is the measurement from the handle to the string. Short brace heights are not forgiving of archer error.

Eye-dominance test.

Before purchasing a bow, you should also test your own hand preference/eye dominance. To determine eye dominance, put one hand over the other with fingers together and thumbs extended to create a small triangular-shaped hole above your two crossed thumbs. Extend your hands toward a target keeping your hands in this position, and slowly bring them toward your face while looking with both eyes at the target. When your hands reach your face, the hole should be in front of your dominant eye. Shooters with dominant right eyes should shoot right-handed (right hand holding the bowstring), and those with dominant left eyes should shoot left-handed (left hand holding the bowstring).

In addition, to choose a bow that's right for you, you'll need to determine your draw length and draw weight. An archery expert at your local sporting goods store will help you determine both. To shoot precisely and accurately every time, you need to select a bow and arrow that fit properly. A beginner should consider selecting a bow that pulls less than forty pounds just until the mechanics of shooting become ingrained. After that, the beginner can move up to the poundage that he can handle and still shoot consistently.

Expected Equipment Costs

You don't have to start with the best archery equipment to experience success in the sport. You can have just as much fun practicing archery with an inexpensive bow, a simple target, and a few arrows as you can with the most expensive, state-of-the-art equipment. But how much money will you need to get started in the sport of archery? The cost depends on the level of archery you want to pursue. You can start off with used equipment, rent equipment from an archery dealer, or buy new equipment, depending on how involved you want to become in this sport. When first learning to shoot a bow, you often can rent the equipment for a few dollars from a local sports store. You can buy beginning equipment for approximately $100 or buy used equipment for about the same cost. If you want top-of-the-line equipment right from the start, you can spend $1500 or more.

Don't let a lack of funds prevent you from pursuing this sport. You can have just as much fun with borrowed, rented, or secondhand equipment as with the most expensive, top-of-the-line archery gear.

Care, Maintenance, and Storage

Over time all archery equipment will require some general, operator-level maintenance. Without proper care and maintenance, your bow and equipment will not perform at their peak levels. However, if you follow some basic steps when caring for your equipment, it should last for many years.

Bow

To keep your bow in good condition, wipe it down thoroughly after shooting it and inspect it regularly. Check the bow handle and arrow rest and make sure these areas are secure and free of any debris or loose materials that might affect your shot. Inspect the length of your bow for any twisting, which may occur when improper storage or transportation put too much stress on the limbs. If you discover a twist that's not too severe, you can fix it with a technique known as *bumping*, which requires you to use a slight amount of force in the opposite direction of the twist.

The most important step in keeping your bow in top working condition is to keep it free of dirt, oil, and liquids. Always keep a clean cloth with you to wipe off any surface material or dampness. Foreign substances on your bow can destroy the finish and allow moisture to seep into the wood. You should also wax your laminate bow with a quality paste wax (like car wax or furniture paste wax) whenever the finish appears dull or damaged. First, gently rub the limbs of your bow with some very low-grade steel wool to smooth the finish and remove any debris. Then, wipe your bow with a clean, dry cloth, and apply the first layer of wax. Finally, when the wax is dry, take the cloth and rub small sections of the bow until you have covered the entire surface and the wax has penetrated into the wood.

Carry and store your bow (and other archery equipment) in a hard case so it won't get damaged easily. Never lean your bow against something or store your bow upright. Keep it in a case when not in use, and hang it vertically or lay it flat. If you don't have a case for your bow, store it in a safe location that allows the bow to rest flat on its side and cover it with a bag or cloth to keep off the dust. Never store your bow (or other archery equipment) in dry heat or excessive

Wiping the bow.

moisture. Many bows are made with layered wood and/or fiberglass parts that are glued together. Exposure to extreme heat or dampness can affect the glue, causing the parts to separate. Look carefully along the edge of your bow and check for cracks and weak spots. Discard bows with separated laminations immediately because these separations compromise the integrity of the bow.

Bowstring and Cables

Waxing your bowstring and/or cables regularly will help prolong their lives. Waxing enables the individual strands of the string to glide smoothly when you draw and release your bow. If your shot sounds unusual, your arrow flies erratically, or your release just doesn't have the right feel, you should try waxing the string. Also, when you're ready to store your bow, wax the bowstring once before you put it away and a second time when you prepare to shoot again.

You can wax your bowstring at any time—even on the field. Just take some bow wax and rub it over the entire length of your bowstring. Then, using your thumb and index finger, rub small sections of the string until you have covered the entire surface and the wax has penetrated into the string. (If you're using a compound bow, follow the same steps to wax the cables.)

You should also examine your bowstring and cables for excessive wear. If the strands between the servings appear fuzzy, the string may have broken fibers, and you'll need to replace the bowstring before shooting again. Next, check the nock point to see if it's clamped tightly to the bowstring. If the nock point is loose, replace it or tighten it with nocking pliers. Also inspect the spot on the bowstring where you place your arrow nock. If this area becomes so worn that it no longer holds your arrows securely, you'll need to replace the bowstring.

Arrows

Always inspect your arrows before shooting them. You never want to put another person or yourself at risk by using damaged equipment (see chapter 4). First, look down the length of the arrow to see if it's crooked. Depending on how much the arrow is bent, you may be able to fix it by bending it in the opposite direction. However, if the bend is severe, you should safely discard the arrow. Next, check for cracks or notches in the shaft. If the shaft is cracked, do not use the arrow anymore. You should also examine the nock for cracks and make sure that both the nock and the point of each arrow are secure. Finally, make sure that the fletchings have not

Inspecting an arrow.

come loose from the shaft. If they have, you can use a small amount of white glue to reattach them.

You can also give your wooden arrows a good coat of paste wax. Apply the wax and allow it to dry thoroughly. Take a clean, dry cloth and rub the wax until it heats up and coats the arrow. Then put the arrow in a spot where the wax can cool and harden. You should wax your wooden arrows before putting them away and store them in an upright position to reduce the effect of gravity on the shaft. If possible, store all your arrows in a hard, protective case.

Archery Safety

Although you can have a great time learning and practicing the sport of archery, remember that a bow is a lethal weapon, and it can do a lot of harm. If you don't take extreme caution with your bow, you can seriously hurt someone else or even yourself. In addition, although you may take precautions when shooting your bow, you need to remain aware of those who might act in an unsafe manner in dangerous shooting conditions.

Don't take chances with your safety. When shooting at an archery range, ask to see the rules. Then follow them. If you have an archery range at home, make up your own rules and make sure that you and any one else who shoots on the range obeys those rules. Also, make sure you are using the right equipment, such as a bow with the proper draw length and draw weight as well as arrows that are the correct length. Too short an arrow can either explode against the bow or get shot through the archer's hand. An archery instructor or a shop employee can assist you in your equipment selection. If possible, shoot with new archery equipment because old equipment can be unpredictable. Wear an arm guard and use a finger tab to protect yourself from injury. And remember to always have proper supervision when learning how to shoot your bow.

Equipment Inspection

Always check your equipment before you warm up with your bow, practice a shot, or aim for the target in competition. Before you nock that first arrow, examine each part of your archery equipment carefully.

Before you shoot, check for these possible problems:

◆ Cracked bow arms: If a crack doesn't get fixed, the bow could break under the tension of your draw and cause an injury.

26

- Loose, broken, or dislocated arrow rest.

- Loose screws or bolts (compound bow).

- Bent S-hooks (compound bow).

- Bent or cracked arrows: Check the nock and arrow for cracks and splinters before you attach the arrow to the bowstring. Break cracked wooden arrows in half, then discard them. If possible, straighten aluminum arrows before you shoot them.

- Cracked or broken nocks: Remove and replace broken or cracked nocks as soon as possible because a damaged nock could slide off the bowstring before you release the arrow. Also, check the condition of the fletchings and the security of the nocks. Loose fletchings can impale the archer's bow hand or arm.

- Poor bowstring condition: If the string looks frayed or if any strand of the string is broken, replace the bowstring immediately before using. A frayed string could break at full draw causing serious injury to you or the archers around you, not to mention the damage it could cause to your expensive equipment.

- Poor bowstring position: Make sure that the bowstring (or bow cables for a compound bow) is positioned properly.

- Unstable nocking point or nock locator.

- Incorrectly set sight.

Splintered wood arrow.

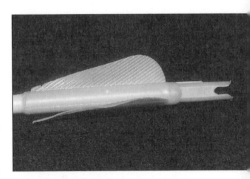

Damaged fletching.

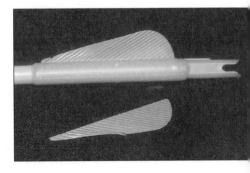

Broken fletching.

Proper Attire

Proper clothing also plays a very important role in archery safety. When dressing to shoot, choose something comfortable and weather appropriate. Also avoid wearing baggy clothing, shirts with long or loose sleeves, clothes with pockets that could get caught on the bowstring, and dangling jewelry, buttons, string, or anything else that could get tangled up in the bowstring.

Safe Shooting

Archery is a safe activity, but every archer may not follow safe practices when participating in this sport. To continue to enjoy archery, you not only must follow general safety rules, but you must also be aware of unsafe archers.

Do's

◆ **Do keep your arrows in a quiver** if possible so that you can pick or sort your arrows easier and more conveniently. If you don't have a quiver, hold the arrows in your hand with the tips in the palm of your hand. Remember that blunt target points can cause injury.

◆ **Do point a nocked arrow to the ground until you get ready to shoot,** and you know for certain that everyone has moved out of harm's way. Make sure to keep your arrow pointed toward the target. Prematurely releasing the arrow can be very dangerous. If you can't draw your bow while pointing it at the target without excessive movement, lower the peak weight of your bow until you can draw it smoothly. As time passes you'll build up your strength enough to pull a heavier weight.

◆ **Do use a bow rack,** if provided.

◆ **Do make sure no one is standing within 30 to 50 yards of the target,** either behind or around it.

◆ **Do nock your arrow under the nock locator.** Don't nock it anywhere else on the bowstring.

◆ **Do tie back long hair.** Long hair could get caught in a bowstring.

◆ **Do wear shoes when shooting** because if you drop an arrow on your bare foot or step on an arrow with your bare foot, you could suffer serious injury.

◆ **Do wear an arm guard and a finger tab** to prevent bruises.

◆ **Do listen to your instructor or leader.**

Don'ts

◆ **Don't try to pull an arrow that slips off the rest back onto the rest** when you've pulled your bow to full draw. You could accidentally shoot it and injure yourself or someone else. Instead, let down your draw and start your shot over again from the beginning.

◆ **Don't try to hold the arrow to the bow with your bow hand.** You could end up shooting your hand, or the arrow tip could injure you.

◆ **Don't shoot arrows straight up into the air.** When they come back down, they could injure you or someone near you.

◆ **Don't shoot at a target that is too small or too thin** to stop an arrow.

◆ **Don't shoot at a target supported by a hard, solid object** such as a rock, a brick wall, or an asphalt street. It may ricochet off the object and hit an unintended target or someone nearby.

◆ **Don't nock your arrow until your instructor tells you to do so.**

◆ **Don't crowd other archers on the shooting line.**

◆ **Don't let anyone with a longer draw length than yours draw or shoot your bow.** Overdrawing the bow could damage it.

◆ **Don't shoot toward a target other than your own.**

◆ **Don't expose your bow to extreme heat.** Excessive heat could lead to limb failure. Never leave your bow in your car for an extended period of time on a hot day.

◆ **Don't *dry fire* your bow.** Drawing and releasing your bowstring without an arrow can severely damage your bow.

Arrow Retrieval

You also must practice safety when retrieving your arrows from the target. Keep the following tips in mind for safely retrieving your arrows.

◆ Step back from the shooting line when you finish shooting with a group or a class—unless someone next to you has pulled his or her bow to full draw. In that case remain in place until he or she has fired the arrow.

◆ Wait for your instructor's permission before you walk to the target. Or wait until all of the other archers in your group have stepped back from the shooting line.

◆ Never run to your target. When running, you could trip and fall and land on the protruding ends of the arrows sticking out of the ground.

◆ Don't leave your bow behind on the ground when walking to the target. Someone could trip over the bow and get hurt.

◆ Pick up arrows that have stuck in the ground as you walk to your target. If the arrow fletching is stuck to the ground, pull the arrow out point first to prevent damage to the fletching.

◆ When retrieving an arrow, place one hand flat on the target and the other hand on the arrow shaft as close to the target as possible.

Safely retrieving arrows.

When pulling arrows from the target, twist them to prevent damaging them. If the arrow sticks, wiggle it slightly until it loosens. If the fletching is buried in the target, cautiously grab the arrow shaft from the back side and pull the arrow through the target.

◆ Make sure that no one is standing behind you when you pull arrows from the target. You don't want to poke someone with the end of your arrow as you retrieve it from the target.

◆ Get someone else to stand in front of the target or prop a bow or quiver on it so no one will try to shoot at that target as you look for arrows that you've overshot.

Strength Training

To shoot an arrow accurately and consistently, you must use precise, controlled movements. You need physical strength in archery not only to draw a bow but also to maintain balance and keep a steady aim. Toning and building your muscles will help you with your coordination, control, consistency, and confidence. Your strength will also determine the poundage of the bow you can use. Using a bow that's too strong for you could possibly damage your muscles and joints. A beginner should use a bow with a light draw weight while learning the basic skills. As the new archer develops skills and physical strength, he or she can then move on to a stronger-weight bow.

You should not begin a physical training program without consulting a physician and/or a trainer first. Moreover, once you determine a program that will work for you, be sure to include some cardiovascular activities to increase the efficiency of your heart and lungs to oxygenate and pump blood throughout your body.

Some archers use progressive loading as a method of strength gaining. Establish your training weight by finding the maximum load that you can lift ten times in repetition. Start with only a few repetitions of each exercise for the first two weeks. Then progressively increase the number of repetitions over a period of four weeks until you can achieve eight to ten repetitions. If a particular exercise causes pain in your muscles or joints, then reduce the weight and the number of repetitions.

Next, you can build strength with specific movements and exercises. The muscle groups used in archery that require strength are the upper-back and shoulder muscles to draw the bow, the shoulder muscles to control the draw arm, the lower- and upper-arm muscles to extend the bow arm, and the finger muscles to hold the bowstring. Also, don't forget

Hammer curl.

Bent-over dumbell fly.

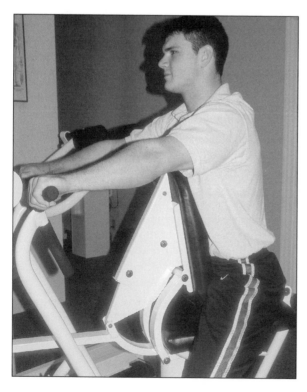

Seated rows.

that when shooting, your leg, hip, trunk, and neck muscles will come into play, helping you control your balance and maintain a steady stance.

To strengthen the muscles you will use in archery, choose exercises that will closely imitate the movements of drawing and shooting a bow. When strengthening these muscles, make sure you work on both the right- and the left-hand sides to maintain a balance of muscle strength.

To develop your muscles properly, you may want to try the following exercises.

◆ To work the muscles in your forearms, do wrist curls and reverse wrist curls.

◆ To strengthen your upper arms, do sets of barbell curls and hammer curls.

◆ To develop the muscles in your shoulders, try lateral raises as well as bent-over dumbbell flies.

◆ To build strength in your back, do bent-over, one-arm dumbbell rows and seated rows with varying elbow elevations.

Stretching

Stretching also plays an important role in archery safety. Neglecting to stretch properly before you shoot your bow could cause you to pull muscles or ligaments. Several factors control the flexibility of joints in the body: bone structure, muscle bulk, tendons, and ligaments. All of these factors control your range of movement.

Before you shoot that first arrow, you need to warm up your body. Many archers have had to give up the sport because of severe shoulder injuries resulting from a lack of "warm" muscles. When shooting a bow, you use muscles that you don't normally use in everyday life, so you'll need to get them ready first.

A resistive exercise band provides an effective way to warm up your muscles before you shoot your bow. The band is coded with different colors according to its tension strength. You can often find resistive bands at local sporting goods stores.

Do the following stretches to warm up your muscles before you shoot and to cool down after you shoot.

◆ To loosen your back muscles, cross your arms in front of your chest and place your hands around your shoulders. Slowly stretch your hands toward the middle of your back. Hold this position for ten seconds.

Stretching with an exercise band.

◆ To stretch your upper-arm and chest muscles, interlock your fingers with your palms facing outward. Extend your arms above your head, keeping your fingers locked. Stretch your arms upward and hold for ten seconds.

◆ To stretch and warm up your chest, tops of your shoulders, and lower arm muscles, bend one arm over your head and down your back. Put the other hand behind your back. Grasp your fingertips and hold on for ten seconds. Then reverse arms and hold the position for ten seconds.

Before you begin practicing archery, keep in mind that a bow is considered a dangerous weapon. Check your local and state laws regarding the transportation and use of your bow and arrow. If you plan to bowhunt or bowfish, contact your state wildlife and fisheries department about proper licensing and season scheduling. If you keep safety a priority, you'll rarely experience any problems. You can safely enjoy archery if you just practice the points we've just discussed.

Archery
Technique

I n some ways archery technique may be compared to home construction. Both progress in a sequence of events. Both need a solid foundation and a dependable structure on which to build. And both result in an outcome that differs in a variety of ways from one to the next. For example, no two homes are exactly alike. Although some structures may have brick walls and marble-tile floors, others may have vinyl siding and hardwood floors. No two archers are alike, either. Some individuals shoot with peep sights and mechanical releases; others may prefer to shoot without these accessories. However, although every builder may use unique plans to manufacture a home, everyone must utilize the same fundamental steps in construction. Similarly, although every archer may develop a distinct shooting style, everyone must follow the same basic guidelines and procedures in archery.

In this chapter you will learn the steps and methods involved for proper shooting, from selecting a shooting stance and nocking an arrow to drawing, aiming, and firing your bow. These techniques are based on generally accepted archery practices. Master these basic steps first, and then you can adjust them to fit your own personal style.

Stance/Posture

A proper stance—your body and foot position as you line up with the target and shoot your bow—is the foundation of your whole shot. No matter what type of bow you shoot, you need to use a stance that gives you stability. If you're not stable, your shot will be awkward and askew. Although posturing styles may differ from person to person, you should always center and evenly distribute your weight. A proficient shooter should take the same comfortable, relaxed, and stable position every time he or she readies for a shot.

If you are new to the sport of archery, you may want to practice shooting with each of the following stances several times before you decide which one is the most comfortable and natural for you. Or, if you participate in a class with an instructor, listen to his or her advice on the best stance for beginning archers.

Regular Stance: If you are right-eye dominant (and your bow arm is your left arm), slide up to the *shooting line* and position the left side of your body toward the target. Stand straight with your feet shoulder width apart and distribute your weight evenly and comfortably. (Keeping your feet in line will bring your shoulders and hips in line with the target.) In the *regular stance*, align your heels and toes so that your toes are even with an imaginary line to the center of the target. Turn your head toward the target. Keep your chin up and look over your left shoulder.

If you are left-eye dominant (and your bow arm is your right arm), slide up to the shooting line and position the right side of your body toward the target. Stand straight with your feet shoulder width apart and distribute your weight evenly and comfortably. Align your heels and toes so that your toes are even with an imaginary line to the center of the target. Turn your head toward the target. Keep your chin up and look over your right shoulder.

Open Stance: By making small changes in the regular stance, archers can use the *open stance.* Adopt a regular stance, then pivot your front foot more toward the target (at approximately a forty-five-degree angle toward the target) and move your back foot forward several inches so that an imaginary line to the center of the target passes through the toes of your front foot and the instep of your back foot. Twist your upper body at the waist to align your shoulders with the target. Remember to roll your weight onto the balls of your feet and lock your knees. This stance will cause you to face the target and use your hips more in the draw.

Closed Stance: To use a *closed stance,* straddle the shooting line and distribute your weight evenly on both feet. Slide the foot that is closest to the target forward a few inches so that an imaginary line to the center of the target passes through the instep of your front foot and the toes of your back foot.

Finger/Hand Placement

You'll need proper finger and hand placement to shoot consistently. Your *bow hand* should hold the bow between your thumb and index

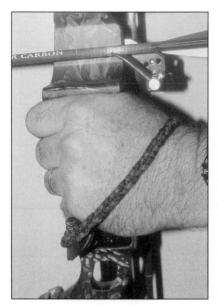

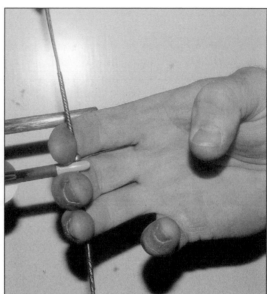

Bow hand finger placement.   **Drawing hand finger placement.**

finger, with only the web and meaty part of your thumb on the bow grip. The palm of your hand should never apply pressure on the bow.

If you choose not to use a release aid, your *drawing hand* should hook the bowstring with your pointer finger above the arrow and your middle and ring fingers below the arrow with the traditional three-finger grip. Your fingers should not touch the arrow because it may slip off the rest if you touch it. If held correctly, the bowstring should fit in the creases of your bottom two fingers and slightly ahead of the crease in your top finger. Attempting to reach the crease in your pointer finger will result in curling your finger around the string, which may cause blisters. Relax your bow hand and keep the back of your drawing hand flat.

Once you feel comfortable with your finger and hand placement, you will need to choose one of three bow-hand positions: low wrist, high wrist, or straight wrist. In the *low-wrist* position, your bow arm lies below your bow hand, with pressure along the inside of your thumb. This position enables your wrist to relax completely and does not require excessive wrist strength to maintain. In the *high-wrist* position, your bow arm extends above your bow hand, with pressure along the inside web of your hand. Although difficult to maintain for long periods of time, a high

Low wrist.

High wrist.

wrist can help reduce bow torque. Finally, in the *straight-wrist* position, your bow arm and bow hand form a straight line, with pressure along your thumb muscle and the inside web of your hand. Although the straight-wrist position can be tire-some to keep up for long periods of time, it is consistent and steady. Practice with the various wrist positions to determine which one fits you best. Base your decision on comfort and ease of use.

Straight wrist.

Bow Arm

The arm that holds the bow is your *bow arm*. (If you are left-eye dominant, your bow arm will be your right arm; it'll be the left arm if you are right-eye dominant.) Hold your bow arm out straight—not tense or rigid—but parallel to the ground rather than bent or curved. When you slide your bow into the "V" made by the fingers and thumb on your bow hand, keep your fingers and your hand relaxed. Their only job is to prevent the bow from falling out of your hand. If you clench your bow hand too tightly, the bow will twist upon release, distorting the flight of your arrow. Also make sure that your elbow moves out of the way of the bowstring and points away from your bow. If your elbow points at the ground, rotate your front shoulder or adjust your bow arm until you've moved your elbow safely out of the way.

Form

Although a newcomer to the sport may not hit the center of the target every time, he or she should remember that consistency in technique is important to becoming a proficient archer. One way to develop and maintain consistency is to use perfect archery form, known as *T-form,* every time you take a shot.

The easiest way to learn T-form is to hold your bow in your bow hand and mimic the motions of making a shot without actually firing an arrow. For example, after you take your stance, raise and extend your bow toward the target and draw the bowstring by pulling your elbow straight back. When you are at full draw, notice that the trunk of your body, your outstretched bow arm, and your draw arm in the holding position create a "T" shape. This T-form alignment is ideal for the proper use of your muscles, the comfort

The T-form.

of your body, and the accuracy of your shot. Hold this position for about five seconds, then gently ease the bowstring forward to its undrawn position. Remember not to dry fire (release the bowstring without an arrow). Dry firing your bow may cause harm to you and/or to your equipment.

Once you are comfortable with T-form, follow the same motions, only this time using an arrow. Nock the arrow below the nock locator on your bowstring with the index feather facing you. Lay the shaft on the arrow rest. With your first finger above the arrow and your second and third fingers below, draw the bowstring and hold your anchor position. Hold this position for about five seconds, then gently ease the bowstring forward to its undrawn position. Practice this motion several times, making sure you are always in perfect form. When you feel comfortable imitating T-form with a nocked arrow, you should be able to incorporate this skill when you finally shoot your bow.

Drawing

Ideally, you should *draw* a bow in one fluid motion. However, to understand the process more completely, you can break it down into four steps.

1. ***Nocking:*** Nocking an arrow refers to the process of placing an arrow nock on the bowstring but also includes all the steps involved with preparing to shoot an arrow. Position an arrow on the arrow rest (or arrow shelf), holding the arrow close to the nock. Keeping the index fletching (or feather) pointing away from the bow, snap the nock of the arrow onto the bowstring under the nock locator (or nock point) to form a ninety-degree angle between the arrow and the bowstring.

2. ***Setting:*** When you've nocked and secured your arrow, set your bow hand on the grip of your bow. Try to grasp the bow exactly the same way every time to ensure con-sistent draw and accuracy. Develop a comfortable and relaxed grip and keep your wrist straight but not rigid. Position your first three fingers around the bow-string, creating a hook. Keep your bow hand relaxed throughout the entire shot. Do not clench the bow.

3. ***Predrawing:*** Raise your bow arm toward the target without raising your shoulder. Lock your bow arm into position and turn your elbow out. (At this point, the elbow of your drawing arm should be near the level of your nose.)

4. ***Drawing:*** Draw the bow back by rotating the shoulder of your drawing arm until your elbow is directly behind the arrow. Although your arm

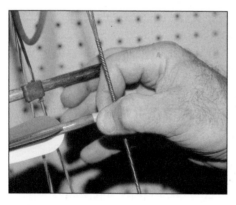

Nocking an arrow.

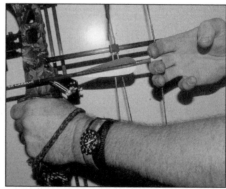

Setting.

muscles do some of the initial pulling, your back and shoulder muscles do most of the work in drawing back and holding the bow. When you draw the bow, try to move one shoulder blade toward the other, feeling the bones and the muscles in your back working to bring your arm, hand, and string toward your face.

Drawing back.

The muscles in your arm and shoulder should remain as relaxed as possible during the draw, lessening the tension in the drawing arm, especially the forearm, which leads to a smoother release. Using your back muscles to draw is also less tiring than using your arm muscles. You should draw the string back smoothly and uniformly and maintain a continuous drawing motion throughout the shot. If you have to use excessive force to pull back the bowstring, the bow probably has too strong a draw weight for you.

When talking about drawing a bow, many archers categorize themselves as either "pushers" or "pullers." Pullers focus on their *draw arms* (the arms that pull back the bowstring), the use of their back muscles, a smooth release, and the follow-through, without worrying too much about their bow arms. Pushers do the opposite. This doesn't mean that each only pulls or pushes; good archers will do both simultaneously but possibly only focus on one motion. Being a pusher or a puller also doesn't mean that one motion takes precedence over the other; generally you have to master both moves to shoot well. If you prefer to concentrate mostly on the draw, try focusing on your bow arm for a few sessions, especially if you've never given it much attention. You may discover that you shoot better by concentrating more on good form in your bow arm rather than worrying about your draw. Even if you find that you shoot better when you focus on your draw, still continue to make sure your bow arm always does the right thing.

A properly anchored arrow.

Anchoring

Anchoring, which is the final stage of the draw, occurs when your drawing hand comes to rest against your face before aiming and releasing. Drawing the string back consistently requires an *anchor point.* Depending on your facial structure and the type of shooting you wish to do, you may use one of several anchor points including drawing the bowstring to your nose, drawing it to your jawbone so that your finger or your thumb touches the corner of your mouth, drawing the string to your cheekbone, or drawing it to your ear. Changing the anchor point or changing your face position will change the forces on the arrow. Therefore, practice to see which anchor point best suits you and try to hold your head in the same position every time to develop a consistent anchor point.

Holding

Holding the bow at *full draw*—with the bowstring pulled back and the draw hand anchored—before releasing the arrow steadies the arrow in position so no extraneous movements affect the arrow's flight. With your back muscles tense, keep your bow arm, draw arm, and elbow in a straight line. In order to steady the arrow, lock your bow arm in place while your string hand rests at your anchor point.

Aiming

Now that you've nocked your arrow and drawn your bow, get ready to aim. Aiming requires concentration and focus on the target but also requires some instinctive abilities. When you look at the spot you want to hit on the target, let your body take over and make the shot in a smooth, fluid motion. You should aim at all stages of the draw. Don't draw and then aim, as the movement will lack smoothness. Instead, aim before you draw and continue to aim during and after your draw.

Some aiming happens instinctively, while other aiming techniques compare sight marks or the point of the arrow with the target. If you are aiming without a bowsight, you should use both eyes (or your dominant eye) and concentrate on the center of the target—the *bull's-eye*. Depending on the target size and the distance from the target, you will need to position the tip of your arrow accordingly. For example, for a 36-inch target face 20 feet away, position the tip of your arrow about 18 inches below the center of the target. However, for distances of 60 feet or more, you may have to line up the tip of your arrow with a spot on the ground, such as a blade of grass, directly in front of your target. With practice you will learn where to position your arrow instinctively for various target sizes and distances.

Most target archers prefer to shoot with a *bowsight*, an aiming device mounted on the bow. Once set properly, this important accessory helps archers position their arrows to shoot at varying distances. If you chose to aim with a bowsight, line up your sight with the bull's-eye. Keep your attention focused on the target, concentrate on where you want the sight, and remember to use good technique. Bear in mind that the sight will most likely move around on the target. Don't try to overcorrect for this consciously; subconscious aiming will do it for you. With practice the sight will stay more or less where you want it, and aiming won't create a problem.

No matter what method you use to aim, remember that the act of aiming should be as unconscious as possible. In other words, if you concentrate too hard on lining up your shot, you most likely will waste too much time and effort holding your bow at full draw. And if you stay at full draw too long, you'll probably make a poor shot because your muscles will start to fatigue. The entire aiming process should only take about ten to fifteen seconds. So, remember to relax and trust your instincts. With practice you will become more accurate and efficient, and aiming will soon become second nature.

Releasing

Releasing the arrow properly is the most important fundamental in archery. The keys to a good *release* include relaxation and concentration. When your bow's at full draw and your bow hand's resting on its anchor point, you've prepared for the release. Continue focusing on the target. Your back muscles should tighten even more before the moment of release. Then you simply let go of all the tension in your fingers and your drawing hand—all at once—while you continue to extend your bow arm toward the target. You need to release the bowstring quickly and gently to prevent any jerking that may affect the arrow's flight. However, because you don't complete the process of freeing the arrow until the arrow has totally left the bow, you should maintain your holding position until the arrow passes the edge of your bow.

Following through

The *follow-through* is far more important to your shot than you may realize. After you release the arrow, keep both of your arms and hands steady. Otherwise the arrow may get off center after the release. When the arrow leaves your bow, your drawing hand should continue its movement along the base of your neck and end up near your shoulder, and your bow

The follow-through.

BASIC ESSENTIALS

arm should continue its extension toward the target. Do not move your eyes from their focus on the target. Following the arrow's flight is not necessary. Keep your follow-through until the arrow reaches the target. Any sudden movements before the arrow hits the target will throw off your shot. Finally, the last step of the follow-through is to relax.

Putting It All Together

Now that you've learned the basics of archery technique, you're ready to put them together to make your first shot. As you step up to the shooting line, remember that mental readiness is just as important as physical readiness. You not only need to concentrate and focus your attention on correct form, you also need to be confident in yourself and visualize a successful shot. You can expect some nervous energy but learn to relax. Let the bow become an extension of your body and make your shot in one fluid motion.

Even though there are no set rules for how you should shoot your bow and arrow, many archers generally accept and use the following sequence of steps:

1. Take your stance.

2. Nock your arrow.

3. Set your bow hand on the grip.

4. Make eye contact with the target.

5. Raise your bow arm toward the target.

6. Draw the bow using proper T-form.

7. Anchor the bowstring.

8. Concentrate and aim for the center of the target.

9. Release the bowstring.

10. Follow through until the arrow hits the target.

Practicing

No matter what methods and techniques you use in archery, the most important factor to becoming a proficient archer is practice. Whether your goal is to hit the bull's-eye once in your lifetime or to win first place in an archery competition, you need to spend some time practicing your newly learned skills. Shooting your bow with your peers under the supervision of an instructor may be the ideal situation for learning and improving. However, if you keep safety in mind and remember to focus on proper shooting technique, you can also practice on your own. Here are a few ideas for putting your archery skills to the test.

Aiming drill: Place a large piece of paper with three bull's-eyes on the buttress. Determine a shooting distance of 10 to 20 yards. Without nocking an arrow, practice drawing your bow, lining up your sight, and aiming at the target. After you steady your sight on the first bull's-eye, move to the second one, and then to the third. Aim for at least five seconds at each bull's-eye, and then gently ease the bowstring back to an undrawn position. Using this drill will help you improve the speed and accuracy of your aim.

Scoring drill: Place a large piece of paper over the target face and draw a tic-tac-toe grid on the paper. Determine a shooting distance of 10 to 15 yards. If you're shooting with others, you can attach small, inflated balloons in each square. The first person (or team) to break three balloons in any tic-tac-toe pattern wins. If you're shooting by yourself, write varying point values in each square and record your points after shooting five ends of five arrows each.

Distance drill: After setting up a bull's-eye target, measure and mark off distances at 20, 30, and 40 yards. Shoot five ends of five arrows at each distance, keeping track of where your arrows hit at each distance. If your arrows drift as you move farther from the target, practice from shorter distances and move outward slowly until you can shoot proficiently at any distance.

Troubleshooting

When you use proper archery form and technique, you'll shoot more accurately, and your arrows will hit the bull's-eye more consistently. However, if your arrows veer off course, you may need to evaluate your shot and look for any mistakes. If you're working with an archery instructor, he or she will be able to guide you. Ask for help if you feel uneasy or unsure about your shot. Also, make sure your equipment is working properly. Sometimes a simple equipment adjustment can make the difference between hitting the bull's-eye and hitting outside the scoring area. If you're practicing by yourself, you can set up a video camera and capture your shooting technique on film. Use the video to analyze your form and make adjustments where needed. The sooner you can spot and correct an error, the better your chances are for overcoming it.

The patterns of your arrows can tell you a lot about your shooting. Directional errors, in which an arrow lands too high, too low, or too far to either side of the bull's-eye, may occur for a number of reasons. Use the following information to help you determine the possible cause of your error and adjust your shooting accordingly.

First, check your equipment to see if . . .

◆ the bowsight is set improperly,

◆ the arrow is nocked wrong,

◆ the nocking point or the arrow rest is out of place,

◆ the upper or the lower limbs of your bow are too stiff, or

◆ the fletching has too much or too little spiral.

Arrows Hit Too High

Arrows hitting the target face above the bull's-eye may be caused by . . .

◆ jerking the bow upward on release,

◆ holding the elbow on the draw arm too low,

◆ shooting too quickly,

◆ tilting your head back too far,

◆ pinching the arrow nock with your fingers,

◆ catching the bowstring on something,

◆ exerting too much pressure with your thumb muscle,

◆ moving your draw hand too far back after release,

◆ overextending your bow arm, or

◆ holding the grip too low.

Arrows Hit Too Low

Arrows hitting the target face below the bull's-eye may be caused by . . .

◆ jerking the bow downward on release,

◆ holding the elbow on the draw arm too high,

◆ bending the elbow on the draw arm too much,

◆ hunching your shoulders,

◆ tilting your head forward,

◆ pinching the arrow nock with your fingers,

◆ catching the bowstring on something,

◆ holding the grip too tightly,

◆ holding the grip too high,

◆ exerting too much pressure with your index finger,

◆ keeping too much tension in the back of your draw hand, or

◆ dipping the bow down during anchor, release, and follow-through.

Arrows Land Too Far Right

Arrows hitting the target face to the right of the bull's-eye may be caused by . . .

◆ twisting your body or moving to the right on release,

◆ bending your wrist outward,

◆ tilting the top limb of the bow to the right,

◆ placing your bow hand too far left on the grip, or

◆ catching the bowstring on something.

Arrows Land Too Far Left

Arrows hitting the target face to the left of the bull's-eye may be caused by . . .

◆ twisting your body or moving to the left on release,

◆ bending your wrist inward,

◆ tilting the top limb of the bow to the left,

◆ placing your bow hand too far right on the grip, or

◆ catching the bowstring on something.

Target Shooting and Archery Competition

Y ou can enjoy archery almost anywhere with just about anyone. You can participate in archery activities with family, friends, schoolmates, and members of archery clubs. And once you have mastered the basics of archery, you can even shoot by yourself. You can test your skills in archery competitions with specific rules and regulations, or you can make up your own games and rules. You can even shoot your bow in your own backyard. This chapter describes how you can find fun and challenging ways to safely practice and enjoy archery and how you can set up an outdoor or indoor range.

Common Archery Activities

Once you learn to proficiently shoot your bow, you may want to test your skills against other archers. Do a little research, and you'll most likely find numerous opportunities to show off your archery skills in local competitions.

The sport of archery has many types of games based around the action of releasing an arrow from a bow to hit a specified target. There are numerous types of archery competitions, from casual to formal events to the Olympic Games.

Three things determine the rules in archery: various associations, types of equipment, and different types of competitions, such as target archery, field archery, clout archery, and so on. Each competition has different rules that the participants must follow.

Target Archery

As a beginner you'll probably start off with target archery before progressing to other types of competition. Target archery tournaments can be held indoors and outdoors. The following are the basic rules of target archery. Most of the major outdoor target archery competitions in the United States follow the same format: a Fédération Internationale de Tir à l'Arc (FITA) Round followed by an Olympic Round.

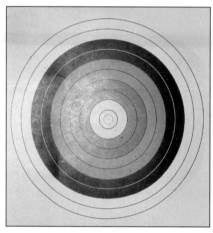

Indoor target.

Archers shoot a specified number of rounds when competing. Each round consists of a certain number of arrows shot from a defined distance. Each arrow that hits the target gets scored accord-ing to its distance from the target's center.

In the FITA Rounds, all competitors compete on one field. Buttresses (target holders) are numbered and pegged securely to the ground. Usually, there are one to three archery targets in each clearly marked lane. The points on the shooting

Outdoor target.

BASIC ESSENTIALS

line directly opposite each buttress must be marked and numbered accordingly. Most archers shoot from a sequence of distances ranging from 30, 50, 70, and 90 meters.

Archery officials may include an organizing committee, a director of shooting and his deputy, a scores committee, scorers (one per target), and a technical commission of at least five members. The archers can compete as individuals and in teams.

Generally, scoring occurs after archers shoot six arrows at pre-determined longer distances and three arrows at predetermined shorter distances. Archers typically call their own scores; then the other archers in the group verify them. The position of the arrow shafts on the target face determines the scores. An arrow that touches two colors or a dividing line on the target scores the higher value. An arrow that passes through the archery target, an arrow rebounding from the *target* (the backing to which a target face is attached), or an arrow rebounding from another arrow will only score if it leaves a mark on the paper or card-board *target face*. An arrow that gets embedded in another arrow (also known as a "Robin Hood") scores the same as the first arrow shot. An arrow that gets de-flected from another arrow scores as it lies in the target. Arrows that hit the target after they rebound from the ground do not score. No archer may touch the arrows or the target face until the scores have been verified. Once the archer pulls the arrows from the target, all holes get marked.

There are two standard circular FITA target faces. One is 122 centimeters in diameter; the other is 80 centimeters. They're divided into ten concentric scoring zones of equal width. The target has five different colors. From the bull's-eye going outward, a shot in each ring counts as 10 points, 9 points, 8 points, 7 points, 6 points, 5 points, 3 points, 2 points, and 1 point. The archer can receive the highest score of ten by shooting an arrow into the two innermost circles. The center of the bull's-eye or bull's-eye ring (*X-ring*) is also scored as a ten and is typically used to break scoring ties. Missing the rings on the target result in a score of zero for that arrow. If you drop an arrow from the bow under any circum-stance, you may pick it up and reshoot it as long as you can pick it up without leaving the shooting line. If you can't reach the arrow from the shooting line, it is considered to be a shot arrow, and you'll get a score of zero.

The Olympic Round is a direct elimination, head-to-head style of competition that takes place at 70 meters. The winner of each match advances until a gold medalist is determined. All archers shoot eighteen arrows at the round's beginning. During the quarterfinals, semifinals, and finals, each archer shoots twelve arrows.

Flight Archery

When participating in flight archery, competitors shoot for distance. Archers use two types of arrows: regular flight and broadhead flight. They can use these arrows in combination with any type of bow. Officials keep records for each combination of bow, arrow, and shooter class. In a flight tournament each archer shoots four *ends* (the number of arrows shot at one time before retrieving them) of six arrows. Each end may be in a different class. The archer can use a different bow for each class, or the archer can shoot the same bow for all four classes.

Clout Archery

Most archers take part in this rarely practiced discipline just for fun. *Clout* archery tests trajectory skill. The target (15 meters in diameter) consists of five concentric circular scoring zones, which are outlined on the ground. The innermost circle is worth five points, and scores decrease to one point in the outermost circle. Each archer shoots thirty-six arrows at the target.

Ski-Archery

Ski-archery combines archery with cross-country skiing. Competitors carry their bows in special backpacks while they ski. The course measures 12 kilometers long for men and 8 for women. Competitors shoot one end of four arrows every 4 kilometers, and during one end the archer shoots from a kneeling position. Targets measure 16 centimeters in diameter and are positioned 18 meters from the shooter. Each shot is a hit or miss. If the archer misses a target, he must ski a 350-meter penalty circuit before leaving the target site. The first athlete to compete the course wins.

Arcathlon

An arcathlon event combines target archery and running. The athlete runs a course and stops at prescribed points to shoot at fixed targets. The typical course measures between 5 and 12 kilometers. Targets measure 16 centimeters in diameter and are positioned 18 meters from the shooter. Athletes make three shooting stops and shoot four arrows at each. The typical event consists of a 1-mile run followed by four arrows shot from a standing position, then another 1-mile run followed by four arrows shot from the kneeling position, then a final 1-mile run followed by four arrows shot from the standing position. Archers can keep their bows at the shooting range, or they can carry them as well.

Field Archery

In this challenging outdoor discipline, the archer takes on the terrain along with the target. The field archery course is set up with twenty-four targets marked with the distance to the shooting line. The distances to another twenty-four targets remain unmarked. The competitors shoot three arrows at each target for a total of 144 arrows. Archers have to make many of the shots uphill or downhill. Field events are held for recurve bow, compound bow, and barebow divisions.

Unique Archery Activities

You can also have fun participating in creative, lighthearted archery activities. Try some of the following ideas or make up your own fun games.

Archery Golf

A popular archery game known as archery golf takes place on a regulation golf course. Archers shoot arrows down the fairway toward each hole, starting at the golf tee and continuing from where the previous arrow landed. The goal is to fire the arrow into a 4-foot circle on the green, level with the golf hole in as few shots as possible over a nine- or eighteen-hole course. You must, of course, first get permission from the golf course management before playing this game on their green.

Archery Darts

The rules for this game are identical to regular darts. Simply create a target face that resembles a dartboard and shoot at it. For a challenge at a similar level to real darts, use a 2-foot, 6-inch target face and shoot 15 yards from the target. There are plenty of fun dartboard games that you can adapt for your bow and arrow.

Swinging Ball

Suspend a soft, rubber ball from in front of a target. Push the ball gently so it swings from side to side and move safely out of the way. Each archer can shoot at the ball from any distance agreed on. To change the level of difficulty, use a smaller or a larger ball.

Outdoor Range Construction

With a little thought and consideration for safety, you can easily set up an outdoor *range* or shooting area. You can use the measurements discussed here to get you started, but keep in mind that these

Target shooting at an outdoor range.

measurements don't conform to the official range sizes and distance for competitive shooting. You can obtain the official range information from the National Archery Association.

First, find an open area with a large, empty space beyond where you plan to place your targets. Make sure you have some type of backstop, such as a dirt mound or a heavily wooded area. You need to know for certain that no one will wander through the area behind the target while you are shooting. Make sure that an arrow you shoot will put no one in harm if it strays far past either side of the target. Even a small twenty-five-pound to thirty-pound youth bow can fire an arrow in excess of 100 yards and can seriously injure someone in its path. Make sure you know your equipment, how it operates, and how to maintain control and safety on the range. After you find a suitable location to set up the range, rope the range off entirely, especially if you are shooting with several people, so that no one has a doubt where the danger zone begins.

Establish your firing line and then make another line about 10 feet behind it. Only allow authorized shooters to stand between the two lines. Make sure no unauthorized person walks in front of the firing line while you or someone else shoots. Place your target line about 25 yards from the firing line. If you step off twenty-five paces, you'll mark off the approximate distance. As your skill level increases, you can move the target back farther. If you've set up your range in an open area, make sure you have at least another 50 yards of open space behind the target to allow for both a safety zone and a recovery area for collecting the arrows that didn't hit the target. (Refer back to the information on arrow retrieval in chapter 4.)

If you construct this range, you'll take on the role of the range master, and you must maintain control of the range at all times while others are shooting on it to make sure everyone has a fun and safe time. If numerous people are shooting or standing around the range at one time, you can use a whistle to maintain order. Designate a specific signal, such as three loud blasts, to notify people of a problem. At this signal everyone should stop in their places and not make another move until the problem gets resolved. You can also let shooters know what to do by announcing instructional phrases, such as "range ready," "shooters to the line," "range clear," "nock and arrow," and "park your bows."

Make sure everyone knows not to cross the firing line once the shooting has started. Also remind the archers to keep all bows and arrows pointed downrange toward the targets at all times.

Indoor Range Construction

You also can set up an indoor range for practice on rainy, cold, or stormy days, but you need to pay special attention to safety and take precaution against any accidental damage caused by misfired arrows. Finding an indoor location with enough room can be difficult. When setting up an indoor range, you can follow the same basic concepts that you used for establishing target and firing lines for the outdoor range. To prevent damaging the floors, lay down easy-to-remove tape to highlight shooting lanes.

Your inside range will need a suitable backstop to stop and catch arrows. Make sure that your backstop is wide enough to catch all renegade arrows. Large blocks of thick Styrofoam and bales of hay work well as backstops behind the targets in an indoor range. You also can use two or more layers of carpet hung behind the targets, but carpet weighs a lot and is hard to store. In addition you may consider using backstop netting, but it usually costs a lot of money. Some archers hang safety curtains slightly away from the walls to catch arrows and to help protect the property. Never rely on curtains to protect personal safety or expensive items or windows, and never allow anyone to pass behind a safety curtain while archers shoot their bows. Also make sure you have a safety area behind the firing line for an indoor range as well.

When shooting at an indoor range, lock all doors that are in the line of fire or that are in the general shooting area. Post warning signs on the outside of the doors alerting everyone that archers are practicing inside.

Depending on the floor type, you may need to protect it from the equipment. Don't lay equipment on the floor that could scratch or puncture it. Use bow racks or side quivers (or self-standing ground quivers) to protect the floor from the arrow points. Also move or protect any furniture or equipment downrange.

For an indoor range you'll follow the same general shooting principles as you follow for an outdoor range.

Archery Targets

You can pay a lot of money for archery targets purchased at specialty shops. So, to save a little money, consider making your own targets. You need to make sure that you construct your target with material tough enough to stop those hard-hitting arrows. What follows are instructions and ideas for making targets at home. Try out several of these targets until you find the one that works best for you.

Straw-bale target: Archers have relied on the straw-bale target for many years. Extremely durable, hay bales can take a lot of arrow hits over a long period of time, and they can stand up to all types of weather. Flax bales work better than other types of straw. This type of hay bale will last longer, and it never seems to decay.

Cloth target: You also can make targets from bundled clothes. You may be able to purchase a bale of unneeded clothes at a local charity thrift store. These clothes are heavy, but they make a large target and cost about $5.00. You can place this target on a wooden pallet after putting it in a tough plastic or cotton sack.

Potato-sack target: Consider constructing a target out of old potato bags and used car tire tubes. To make this target cut old tire tubes into small strips of about 2.5 centimeters by 10 centimeters (1 inch by 5 inches) and pack them tightly into the potato sack. You should use three sacks together for better results. When the target becomes unusable due to damage, simply transfer the rubber strips to a new bag. You can easily remove arrows from this weather-resistant target. And you only have to change the bags once in a while because the rubber strips will last a long time. As time passes, you may want to add more rubber strips to replace the older ones.

Tarp target: For this target you'll need a feed sack or a similar bag and as many old tarps as you can find. Take one tarp and fold it tightly enough to fit inside an old sack. Then, stuff the sack with more tarps until you can't fit any more. Seal the bag using any method you like. This easy-to-make, cheap target will stop arrows from as close as 5 or 10 yards.

National Archery Associations

For more information on archery competition, regulations, and organizations, consider contacting one or more of the following:

Fédération Internationale de Tir à l'Arc (FITA)
avenue de Cour 135
CH1007 Lausanne
Telephone: 41 21 6143050
E-mail: info@archery.org

International Field Archery Association (IFAA)
Web site: www.archery-ifaa.com
E-mail: archery@dtgnet.com

National Archery Association (NAA)
One Olympic Plaza
Colorado Springs, CO 80909
Telephone: (719) 866–4576
Web site: www.USArchery.org

National Field Archery Association (NFAA)
Route 2, Box 514
Redlands, CA 92373
Telephone: (800) 811–2331
Web site: www.nfaa-archery.org

Glossary

Anchor point: The point on the body where the draw hand is positioned during a shot.

Arm guard: Leather or plastic device worn on the inside of the bow arm to protect the forearm from the bowstring when it's released.

Arrow rest: A small, tablike shelf where the arrow rests.

Arrow shelf: The small shelf where the arrow sits when the archer aims, draws, and releases the arrow.

Back: The side of the bow facing away from the archer and toward the target.

Bow arm: The arm that lifts and holds the bow.

Bow hand: The hand that holds the bow.

Bowsight: A device mounted on the bow that enables an archer to aim at a target.

Bowstring: The chord to which the arrows are fitted, usually constructed of Kevlar or Dacron.

Bow window: The recessed area above the bow handle or grip.

Bull's-eye: The center area on the target face that has the highest scoring value.

Bumping: A bow-maintenance technique that requires a small amount of force in the opposite direction of a twist in a bow to "bump" it back into the correct form.

Cam: A small, oval-shaped wheel mounted on each tip of each limb of a compound bow.

Closed stance: Shooting stance in which an imaginary line to the center of the target passes through the instep of the front foot and the toes of the back foot.

Clout: Long-distance competitive shooting using a target positioned flat on the ground.

Compound bow: A bow with a cable system and an eccentric pulley at each limb tip.

Crest: Colored bands or markings close to the fletchings.

Draw: To pull the bowstring back.

Draw arm: The hand that draws back the bowstring.

Drawing hand: The hand that draws back the bowstring.

Draw length: The distance between the nocking point on the bowstring and the grip of a bow at full draw.

Draw weight: The number of pounds of pull required to draw back a bow.

Dry fire: Releasing the bowstring without firing an arrow, possibly damaging the bow.

Eccentric pulley: Located on each tip of the limb of a compound bow to provide archers with let-off.

End: The designated number of arrows shot at one target before scoring and retrieving.

Face: The side of the bow facing the archer.

Field archery: Competitive outdoor shooting, usually in a wooded area with a variety of target distances and sizes.

Finger tab: Leather or plastic device worn over the fingers on the draw hand to protect the draw fingers and ensure a smooth release.

Fletching: Feathers or vanes at the rear of an arrow that guide and stabilize the arrow during flight.

Flight: An individual feather that makes up part of the fletchings.

Follow-through: The archer's continued motion and holding position after releasing the arrow; important for shot accuracy.

Full draw: Position in which the bowstring is drawn back and the draw hand is anchored, ready to release the arrow.

Handle/grip: The place between the two bow limbs where the archer holds the bow.

High wrist: Bow hand holding position in which the wrist is level with the top of the bow arm.

Holding: Maintaining a steady position while aiming at full draw.

Index feather: The feather on the arrow shaft that is mounted at a right angle, usually a distinct color.

Kisser button: A small disk on the bowstring that makes contact with the archer's lips at full draw to ensure consistency of anchor and head positions.

Let-off: The weight reduction from a compound bow's peak weight to its holding weight.

Limb: Part of the bow from the riser to the tip.

Longbow: A bow with no recurve; widely used in Europe during the Middle Ages.

Low wrist: Bow hand holding position in which the hand is placed flat against the bow handle.

Nock: The plastic piece on the end of an arrow that fits onto the bowstring; to place an arrow on the bowstring for a shot.

Nocking point: The place on the bowstring where the nock locator is found and the arrow is fitted.

Nock locator: The place on the bowstring marked to let the archer know where the arrow nock is placed.

Open stance: Shooting stance in which an imaginary line to the center of the target passes through the toes of the front foot and the instep of the back foot.

Peep sight: A plastic or metal piece with a small hole through which an archer looks when lining up and aiming at a target.

Pivot point: The place where you grip a recurve bow between your thumb and the rest of your fingers.

Point: The sharp end of the arrow that penetrates the target.

Quiver: Any device that holds arrows.

Range: A location for shooting; the distance to be shot.

Recurve: The forward curves on the limb tips of a recurve bow.

Recurve bow: A compact bow with forward-curving limb tips.

Regular stance: Shooting stance in which an imaginary line to the center of the target passes through the toes of both feet.

Release: To let go of the bowstring and propel the arrow.

Release aid: A handheld device that attaches to the bowstring and aids in the drawing and releasing of the bowstring.

Riser: The handle area of the bow.

Shaft: The body of an arrow.

Shooting line: A marked line parallel with the targets where archers position themselves to shoot.

Sight: A mechanical device placed on the bow with which the archer can aim at the target.

Stabilizer: An additional weight added to the face or the back of the bow's handle riser to minimize the torque of the bowstring on release.

Stabilizer insert: Place where a stabilizer or weighted rod can be attached to the bow.

Stance: Body and foot position used to line up with a target and shoot a bow.

Straight-wrist: Bow hand holding position in which the bow arm and bow hand form a straight line.

Target: The backing to which a target face is attached.

Target face: The paper or cardboard scoring face.

T-form: The ideal shooting form in which an archer's body, bow arm, and draw arm resemble a "T" shape.

Torque: A clockwise or counterclockwise rotation of the bow handle upon release of the bowstring.

Tuning: Adjustments made to archery equipment to ensure perfect arrow flight.

X-ring: The small scoring circle in the center of a bull's-eye, often used as a tie breaker.

Index

Authors Beth Habeishi (left) and Stephanie Mallory.

About the Authors

Beth L. Habeishi is a communication arts professor and a freelance writer, editor, and outdoor photographer. She has written numerous articles in a variety of local and national publications and has enjoyed the sport of archery for many years.

Stephanie Mallory, the public relations coordinator for Jordan Outdoor Enterprises, has published numerous articles and photographs nationally as a freelance writer and photographer. She spends her leisure time practicing her archery skills.